THE TRAPPER'S BIBLE

Traps, Snares, and Pathguards

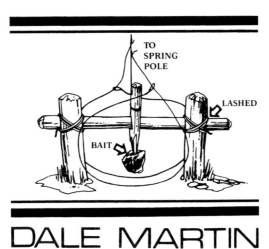

TO SPRING POLE

LASHED

BAIT

DALE MARTIN

PALADIN PRESS
BOULDER, COLORADO

Also by Dale Martin:

Into the Primitive: Advanced Trapping Techniques

The Trapper's Bible: Traps, Snares, and Pathguards
by Dale Martin

Copyright © 1987 by Dale Martin

ISBN 13: 978-0-87364-406-8

Printed in the United States of America

Published by Paladin Press, a division of
Paladin Enterprises, Inc.,
Gunbarrel Tech Center
7077 Winchester Circle
Boulder, Colorado 80301 USA
+1.303.443.7250

Direct inquiries and/or orders to the above address.

PALADIN, PALADIN PRESS, and the "horse head" design
are trademarks belonging to Paladin Enterprises and
registered in United States Patent and Trademark Office.

Visit our Web site at www.paladin-press.com

Contents

iii

Preface

There is a variety of more modern traps available in the world today. Everything from a zillion sizes and variations of the standard old steel trap to box-type capture traps made by companies like Hav-A-Hart and a hundred others. So, why snare?

One reason is the initial cost. The cost of standard steel traps and, especially, commercially made box-type traps is fairly high. More so, if you buy six or eight at a time.

Conversely, all of the snares and traps described in this book are homemade from a variety of around-the-house-type stuff. In almost none of the traps shown will you have to buy anything to make it, if you just halfway try in the scrounging-around department. For a few of the designs, you might have to spend a little, like 50¢ for a piece of electric wire to make a rabbit snare, or something else equally cheap. The initial cost of all the traps in this book is virtually nil.

Another reason that someone might have for going into this type of primitive, but effective, trapping is to poach on his neighbors' land. If you happen to be one of those old boys who likes to occasionally take a food animal or a fur-bearer off his neighbors' land, snaring might come to your aid in a number of ways.

First, financially. If you set a steel trap on your neighbors' land and he happens to find it and pick it up, you've lost from about five to twenty dollars, depending on the size of the trap. Whereas if he picks up a rabbit snare you've set, you've lost nothing. Even if you had to buy (heaven forbid!) the small copper wire you made the snare with, you have only lost a few cents.

Second, and perhaps more importantly, if your neighbor finds a conventional spring-type steel trap, you can bet he's going to know what it is and that someone is trying to trap on his land. More than likely, he is going to be mad enough to do his absolute best to try to catch you. At the very least, he is going to watch his land more closely from then on, which will hamper your comings and goings to some degree.

On the other hand, if he finds a snare you have set, he may not even know for sure what it is. Probably 90 percent of the people in this country have never seen one.

Third, snares are darn near impossible to spot in the woods, unless you are an old pro who really knows what to look for. They look too much like a natural part of the environment when set. And they can be camouflaged even more so if necessary. Unless a snare is set directly on a path, such as a large animal snare would be, most people will walk by without noticing it.

Another thing to think about concerning the material in this book is that during some great social upheaval or economic breakdown, there might not be any modern traps available, or any money to buy them if there were. During the aftermath of a war, or even a collapse of the monetary system as in 1929, this type of primitive trapping might come in handy.

But, for the most part, my own personal interest in this subject is none of the reasons I have listed. Many people simply enjoy the outdoor lore of living off the land—or, at least, feeling as if they *could* survive if they really had to do so. It gives one a sense of worth and measure of self-reliance.

I enjoy the conveniences of my home and the ease of buying food at the store. And as long as I can do so, that is what I intend to do. But in the back of my mind, when I come across a new piece of outdoor lore, I file it away. You never know in this old world.

D.M.

1987

Introduction

The main subject of this book is snares, although a variety of other traps will also be shown. First, we will go through the mechanics of small wire snares and large animal snares. Then, we will look at some transplant traps for moving animals from one area to another without harming them.

Some camp or path alarms to warn you of a possible intruder are also included, along with some deadly path-guarding traps that should never be used except in a desperate situation to save your own life. Refinements of these various snares and traps will be shown, as well as a number of simple variations of most designs.

Lastly, I have provided a listing of some sources for more modern products in this and related fields, as all of the snares and traps shown in this book are of a primitive or homemade design.

The first thing that you must realize about snaring is that *snares do work*, and they work well.

We have all seen, in old movies on television, the old cowboy in the desert who has lost his food and supplies, and probably even his horse, in a shoot-out with the bad guys. A hundred miles from any help, it looks like starvation is just around the corner.

So, what does the old boy do? They never show you. The next scene you see is the ever-resourceful cowboy picking up a nice, plump rabbit that has what looks like a shoelace around its neck, with the other end of the shoelace tied to a mesquite bush. (Where did he get a shoelace, anyway? He's wearing boots!)

They leave you with the definite impression that all the old boy had to do was stumble out from camp a few feet, tie a string to a bush, make a loop on the other end, and the rabbits started fighting to see who could be the first to get caught in the loop.

In the next scene, the cowboy is back at the campfire, munching on a nicely cooked rabbit leg, and he has survived another adventure. Yeah, sure.

Most people, seeing such a movie, might think something on the order of "who do they think they're kidding?" or "makes a good movie, but. . ." Any halfway reasonable person who saw such a movie version of snare use would have so many questions about how the snare worked that he would tend to disbelieve in its use completely.

What makes the animal get into the snare in the first place? What keeps the line snubbed up tight on the animal? How does it always catch the animal right on the throat? Does it always catch on the throat? Why can't the animal get out of it? What is the line made of? All these questions would make most people think "snares are another one of those things like silencers on a gun; they work great in movies, but not nearly so well in real life."

Snares do work. Nothing much like the episode I have just described, but they do work. In most cases, 90 percent of what we see in movies is garbage. Also, about the same percentage of what we hear from others about obscure subjects like trapping is also garbage.

But, hang in there. Read this book; especially the description in Chapter One of the "pest" snare. Master it and its variations, and you will have mastered at least the basics of snaring. And it's easy. Any klutz can learn to set snares for a variety of game. I know—I'm about three-quarters klutz myself.

As with most things, you absolutely *must* get the basic details correct. You *have* to use appropriate line material. You *have* to set the trigger properly. When setting unbaited snares, you *have* to set the snare in the right location. Details count. But, like I said, it's easy.

Remember, chapter one alone will tell you a lot about basic snaring, and since snaring is almost on the order of a lost art, I hope you will learn the secrets of this book. Enjoy!

Chapter 1

Pest Snares

I call the first snare presented a "pest" snare, not because that is the only thing it is good for, but because that is what I use it for. Most people would call it a rabbit snare, if they use the unbaited version set at the hole into a rabbit warren.

It is good for almost any animal up to the size of a large house cat, although your neighbors may get upset if you use it for that, and catch their tabby. It is excellent for rabbits and game of equal size. It might take a small fox, although that would be a bit chancy. Usually, heavier line is needed for anything larger than rabbit-size game.

First, you need about a two-foot piece of 18-2 appliance wire. (You can use any size close to this; 16-2 would be fine also.) This type of wire is extremely common lamp-cord wire and can be found in almost any lumberyard or hardware store. If you shop at a high-priced outlet, a two-foot piece of this wire might cost you fifty cents, at the most.

Odds are, if you scrounge around a little, you can find some wire of this type around the house, storage building, or garage. A broken lamp or any such appliance that is unrepairable will provide you with the needed wire.

5

This type of wire has two halves, each with insulation covering an inner core of copper wire. Split the two halves of the insulated wire so that you now have two two-foot pieces of the wire with the insulation still attached.

Next, using a pair of pliers and a knife to get it started, peel the insulation off the inner core of the soft fibers of copper wire on each of the two pieces. There should be 40 or 50 small, hair-like strands of copper inside the insulation of each of the two-foot pieces. Take care not to tangle up the copper strands as you peel off the insulation.

Now, you should have two two-foot pieces of copper wire. Each piece should have approximately 40 to 50 strands in it. The insulation, at this point, is gone.

Next, divide the strands in each two-foot piece by half, again being careful not to tangle them. You should now have four two-foot pieces of wire, with each piece having 20 to 25 strands in it. (If you used a scrounged piece of wire from an old lamp and it was of a size so that you ended up with a few less strands or a few more, don't worry about it. As little as 15 strands will be okay for rabbit-size game, and as many as 30 strands won't be too many. However, I find that 20 to 25 strands is about ideal.)

Now, take one of the four pieces and twist the wire slightly so that it becomes more tightly woven into a single strand, rather than 20 to 25 strands of copper just lying together loosely. The more tightly woven single strand should be about the size of a pencil lead, maybe half again larger.

Next, evenly cut off the ends of the piece you are working with and twist the ends so that they will not unravel easily.

Now, follow the previous two steps on the other three pieces of wire that you have.

Note: To avoid confusion, please note that out of one piece of two foot long 18-2 (or similar) lamp cord wire, we end up with enough material to make four snares of this small size. How's that for economy?

At this point, you should have four pieces of wire two feet long, each with 20 to 25 strands of wire, each cut off evenly on the ends and twisted together fairly well—the makings of four identical snares.

Now, put a loop on each end of each piece of wire. The loop on both ends of each wire should be about the size of a dime. One loop will serve as the connection to the spring-pole mechanism, and the other will form the lasso itself.

Now, run one loop through the other to form the snare lasso on each of your four snare wires. Draw up the loop on each wire that forms the lasso so that the wire will have just enough room to slide through when put under tension (see Figure 1).

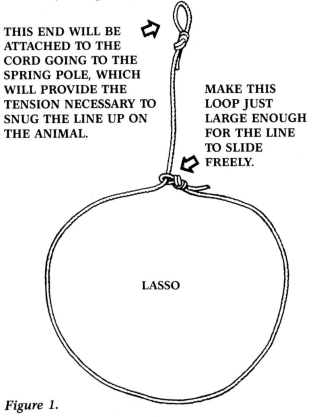

THIS END WILL BE ATTACHED TO THE CORD GOING TO THE SPRING POLE, WHICH WILL PROVIDE THE TENSION NECESSARY TO SNUG THE LINE UP ON THE ANIMAL.

MAKE THIS LOOP JUST LARGE ENOUGH FOR THE LINE TO SLIDE FREELY.

LASSO

Figure 1.

At this point, let's forget that we have four pieces of wire and concentrate on one. Obviously, we do not have to set four snares right off the bat simply because we have the materials. Save the other three pieces of wire for later.

You should now have a wire snare with the lasso already formed as shown in Figure 1.

The next step is to locate a good springy tree to use as a spring pole. The spring pole is what jerks the line taut around the animal once the trigger is tripped. The small sapling you choose for a spring pole will have to be springy enough so that when it is bent over, it will retain its tendency to pop back up when released. This is a very important detail. Some small saplings, when bent over, will quickly lose their tendency to pop back up. You can usually tell just by the feel of the return pull when you bend one over whether it will be satisfactory or not. If you are undecided on a potential spring pole, bend it over several times. If it does not snap back up quickly to an upright position, it will not do.

Finding a good spring pole (and it's usually not hard) will dictate the exact location of this snare, as this particular snare is a baited trap which does not have to be on a trail or at the entrance to the animal's den.

Attach a piece of almost any type of cord (I use fairly heavy trot line cord) to the tip of the spring pole. You will probably have to trim some or even most of the limbs out of the way on the spring pole itself.

Pull down on the cord that you have just attached to the spring pole to a point where the pole is exerting only enough back pull that you think it would jerk a four- or five-pound weight off the ground if the cord were released suddenly.* At this point, make sure your cord

*If you set the spring pole so that it is exerting by far too much pull, it will be harder to trip the trigger. A little variance will not matter, but do not set the spring pole overly strong. Test the pull with a four- or five-pound weight tied to the end of the spring-pole cord if you desire.

will reach to within an inch or so of the ground. Cut off any excess.

Next, whittle a peg from a tree branch to use as a trigger as shown in Figure 2. You will also need to drive a stake into the ground with a nail in it as part of the trigger. Again, see Figure 2, and for trigger details, see Figure 3.

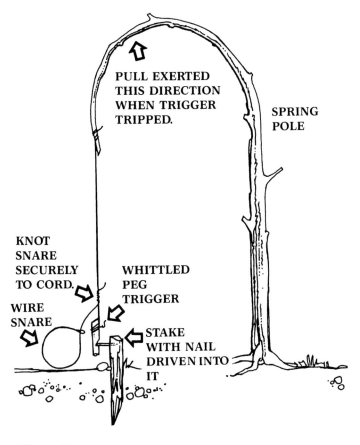

Figure 2.

Next, tie the wire snare to the cord going to the spring pole, and set the trigger as shown in Figures 2 and 3.

In studying Figures 2 and 3, it should be apparent that

any slight tugging on the snare lasso by an animal trying to get through it would bump the peg off the nail. Up would go the spring pole, tightening the wire lasso on the animal, catching the animal.

Also, as in Figure 3, it should be apparent that because of the nature of the wire we are using, the loop will hold

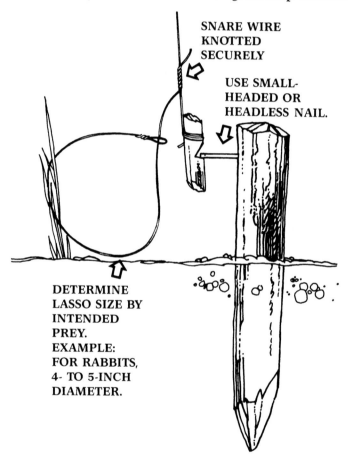

SNARE WIRE
KNOTTED
SECURELY

USE SMALL-
HEADED OR
HEADLESS NAIL.

DETERMINE
LASSO SIZE BY
INTENDED
PREY.
EXAMPLE:
FOR RABBITS,
4- TO 5-INCH
DIAMETER.

Figure 3. **If necessary, use grass or small weeds to hold the snare in the desired position. Little else will be needed. The stiff nature of the copper wire will allow it to almost stand by itself, yet it is small in diameter, pliable, and strong enough to hold the game once caught.**

itself open, and very little grass or weeds will be needed to hold it up. Once tripped, the cutting nature of the copper wire will keep it snubbed tight around the animal so that, in most cases, it cannot get out.

Now, before we get too far down the line in snare-setting, you need to decide just why you are setting this snare. It will make a difference in how you continue.

One reason someone would set snares is for food for simple survival, or to supplement the family table. The other most common reason for snare-setting is for the hide of the animal. One might set snares for animals merely to collect the hide of fur-bearing animals, which could be sold to fur buyers for the good old American dollar.

In the first case, in search of food, you want to set the snare so that it will not kill the animal if at all possible. Simple logic will tell you that if you set a snare for rabbit (or whatever) and catch one in the first hour or two, by the time you come back the next morning, the meat will be spoiled if the snare kills the animal.

Of course, this would not apply if you checked the set every hour or two, but usually one cannot check a set that often. So, in the case of snaring for food, you want the animal to still be alive when you get to it.

In the second case, if you are merely selling the hides of caught animals and have no interest in the meat, you would probably *prefer* that the snare set kill the animal to reduce the chances of the animal ruining its pelt in many hours of struggling against the snare.

In each of the two instances listed, the snare is set *slightly* differently to bring about the desired result.

It must be noted that in both cases, there is no sure thing in setting snares. When you set a snare to kill the animal it catches, sometimes it will not do so. Also, when you set a snare to merely hold an animal, sometimes the animal will die. Snares are primitive and cannot be completely controlled to this fine of a degree. What follows will help you set them so that they will perform as you desire the majority of the time.

The change in the setting is done with the spring pole. Assume that you are after food in a case of simple survival. The animal you are attempting to snare is in the four-pound range. Now, simple logic will tell you that the farther you bend over the spring pole when setting the trigger, the more force it is going to have jerking up when the trigger is released. Or, vice versa, if the pole is bent over only slightly during the set, its pull strength on the snared animal will not be nearly so great. Thus, the same spring pole can be set for a variety of pull strengths depending upon how far over toward the ground you bend it in the setting of the snare.

So, in the example of snaring for simple survival food, set the pull strength of the spring pole so that it will *not quite* pull the four-pound animal you are seeking off the ground. The reason for this is that if the snare catches the prey directly on the throat and lifts the animal completely off the ground, it will die very quickly, and the meat will be spoiled if you do not get back to the snare within a fairly short period of time. Yet, at the same time, the spring pole needs to exert enough pull on the snare to keep the line snubbed up tight on the animal.

In the second case, where you merely want the hide of the animal, set the spring pole so that the four-pound animal will be held helpless in the air once caught. If the snare happens to catch the animal directly around the neck, it will kill it, but in this scenario you will not care.

In both cases, as stated before, the end result is not always perfect. In the "for food" case, sometimes the animal will die in your snare regardless of what you do—not often, but at least part of the time.

In the second case, the snare *quite often* will not kill the animal. It usually will not kill the animal unless it catches the animal around the neck. (Snares rarely do this. The animal is usually about half way through or at least has one of its front legs through before the snare trips.) However, if it is set so that the animal is held off the ground, helpless in the air, it *will* minimize the pelt destruction of a struggling animal.

Please note that if you are setting the snare for just anything that comes along, this refinement will not apply. This technique works on the principle of knowing in advance the approximate size (weight) of the intended animal. If you are setting a snare in an area where it might catch a two-pound animal or a ten-pound animal with equal likelihood, you will just have to set the snare for an average size and hope for the best.

Now, back to our original snare set. By now, in reading and studying the illustrations, it should be evident that an animal trying to pass through the lasso would probably (nothing in this world is a sure thing) spring the trigger and be caught. But, how do you get the animal to walk right into this trap?

Two ways. The first requires little explanation. You set the snare at the entrance to the animal's den hole so that it will snare the animal in its natural comings and goings. The second way, and the one we will discuss in this set, is with bait.

There are probably a lot of good ideas floating around out there for setting snares with bait. The system I always use is this: using whatever is available (two-by-fours, sticks, logs, whatever), I build a "box canyon" on the ground with the bait at the closed end and the snare set at the open end. For example, if I am in the woods away from other materials, I can usually find a log like you might scrounge up to use in a campfire. I pile up two or three such logs, usually a foot or so tall, put the bait in the boxed end, and cover the top to form a lid. This sounds like a lot of work, and a problem to find the materials, but it's really not. See Figure 4.

TRIGGER REFINEMENTS

I probably will not live long enough to write a book long enough to put down all the variations of the above-mentioned simple snare. There are most likely thousands

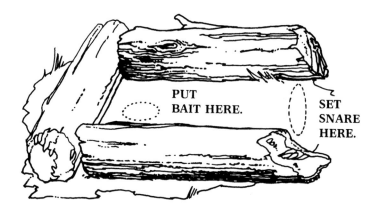

PUT
BAIT HERE.

SET
SNARE
HERE.

Figure 4. To set up this "box canyon" (shown from above), (a) set up three logs (or anything else) to form a box canyon, (b) set bait and snare, and (c) then lightly cover the top of the bait pen with sticks. Note: this works almost as well without cover, but use cover when materials are available.

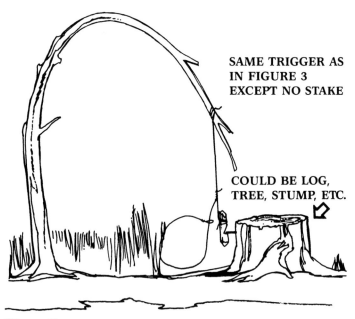

SAME TRIGGER AS
IN FIGURE 3
EXCEPT NO STAKE

COULD BE LOG,
TREE, STUMP, ETC.

Figure 5.

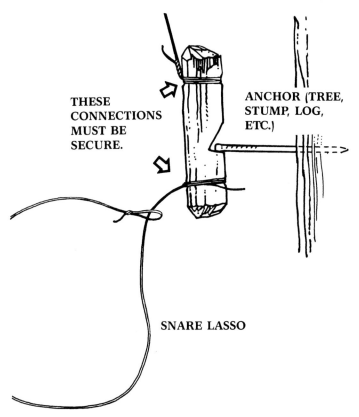

THESE
CONNECTIONS
MUST BE
SECURE.

ANCHOR (TREE,
STUMP, LOG,
ETC.)

SNARE LASSO

Figure 6. **This variation of Figure 5 provides a very fine trigger, easily tripped.**

of variations on snaring. However, you need to know as many as you can absorb. We will consider a dozen or so refinements and variations of this basic snare.

First, let us consider the trigger. The one used in Figure 3 is the most simple one I know of that can be used in almost any situation, but it could be even easier in certain instances.

Suppose there is a tree or log (even the log on your bait pen), stump, or similar object. You could drive the nail into it and you would not have to have a stake to drive into the ground. The easiest way to show the trigger or other variations is to include here the following self-explanatory illustrations.

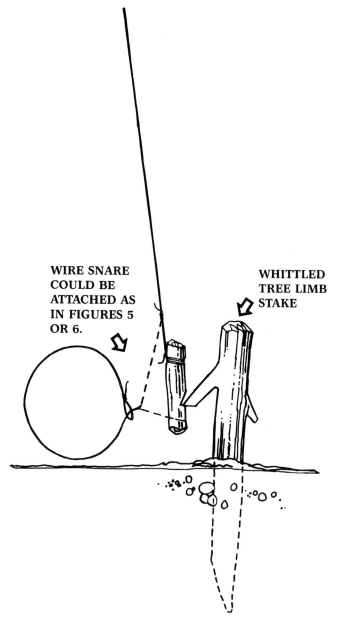

WIRE SNARE
COULD BE
ATTACHED AS
IN FIGURES 5
OR 6.

WHITTLED
TREE LIMB
STAKE

Figure 7. **Use this setup when only primitive materials are available.**

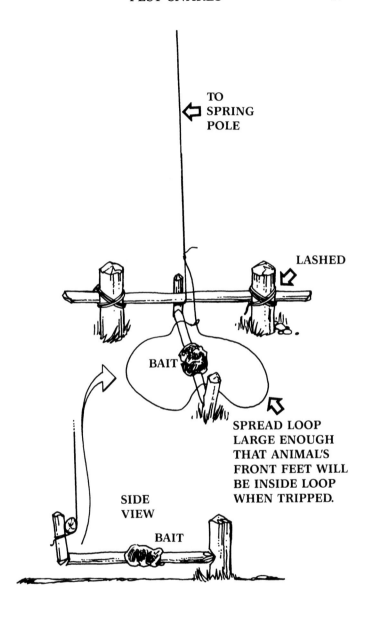

Figure 8. This variation changes both the trigger and bait placement from our original design.

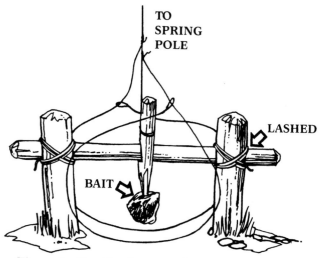

Figure 9. For the front and back snare, use two snare lassos, one on each side of the bait.

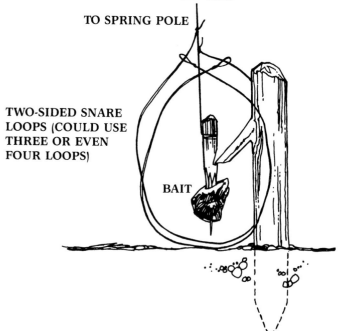

Figure 10. This is a variation of the trigger in Figure 7, except the whittled peg is longer and is used for bait placement.

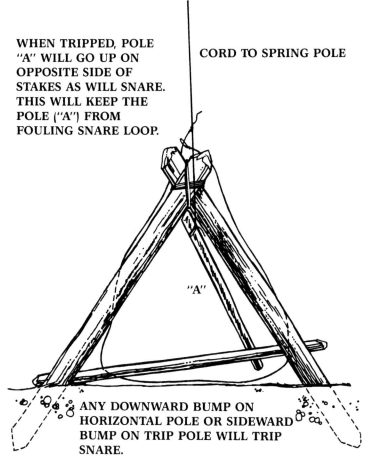

WHEN TRIPPED, POLE "A" WILL GO UP ON OPPOSITE SIDE OF STAKES AS WILL SNARE. THIS WILL KEEP THE POLE ("A") FROM FOULING SNARE LOOP.

CORD TO SPRING POLE

"A"

ANY DOWNWARD BUMP ON HORIZONTAL POLE OR SIDEWARD BUMP ON TRIP POLE WILL TRIP SNARE.

Figure 11. This trip bar snare is used most often on an animal path or at a den entrance.

SNARING REFINEMENTS

There are several little things you can do after you get the basic concept of snaring down pat. These little "tricks of the trade" will enhance your snaring success ratio. We will now consider several of these refinements.

The first will be a little trick with the wire lasso itself that will help it to snap closed when jiggled only slightly. Figure 12 shows the small wire lasso that we have pre-

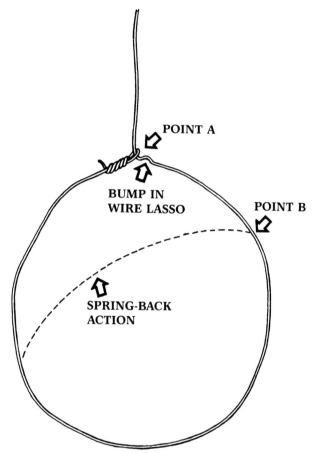

POINT A

**BUMP IN
WIRE LASSO**

POINT B

**SPRING-BACK
ACTION**

Figure 12.

viously made—we have already seen some variations in its use. There is a slight bump in the wire lasso just below the lasso loop.

Assume that the lasso is formed, not as you see it, but at the dotted line juncture at point B. If it is formed thus and you pull the loop back so that it rests on the small bump in the wire you have formed at point A, the wire will be stiff enough that it will snap back to its dotted line position with just barely a touch.

What this does is help the snare close on the animal *even before* the trigger is tripped and insure that the trigger *will be* tripped. The wire from point A to point B should be as smooth and bump-free as possible to facilitate this spring-back action. This little refinement takes a little practice and is not easy to master, but it will increase your snaring production.

Another refinement concerns making the trigger trip a little quicker than it would normally be. Run a thread or similar small string from the trigger to the snare wire. The technique and purpose will be obvious as displayed in Figure 13.

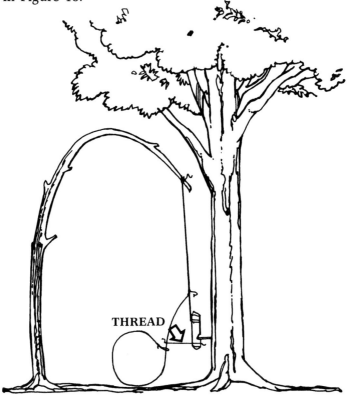

Figure 13. **In the thread trip snare, a small thread located strategically will assist the trigger in tripping more quickly.**

Another little variation, although not really a refinement, involves using a loop on the end of your spring-pole cord, and a string looped around it to trip the trigger. In this way, you can set this trigger without whittling the peg release. See Figure 14.

The next release carries this system one step farther. See Figure 15.

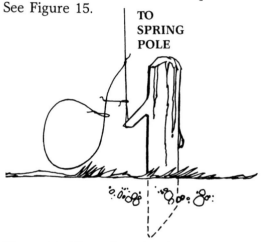

TO SPRING POLE

Figure 14. **The principle of this setup is that the string loop will pull the spring pole cord loop off the peg. Note that the loop at the arrow must be set very finely and the spring pole strength must not be too hard, or this set will be difficult to trip.**

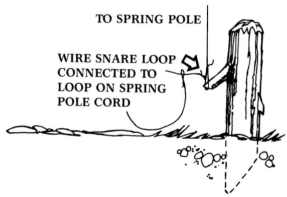

TO SPRING POLE

WIRE SNARE LOOP CONNECTED TO LOOP ON SPRING POLE CORD

Figure 15. **As in Figure 14, the loop at the arrow must be set finely and spring pole strength cannot be too strong.**

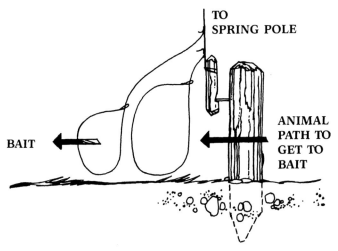

Figure 16. This double snare is excellent for "box canyon" use, as in Figure 4. The principle of this setup is that one larger loop and one smaller loop, set as shown above, provide more chance of a successful snare if the animal must come in from a predetermined direction.

OTHER SNARE VARIATIONS

Now, we will consider variations in other areas. For example, the spring pole. Let's say there is no handy sapling around where you wish to set your snare. Instead, you can find a spot where you can utilize a tree limb for a spring-pole substitute.

You need some upward pull. Even if there is no spring pole, you can accomplish this upward motion by using the downward pull of a falling weight.

Figure 17 shows you how to use a weight and some rope or cord in place of a spring pole. (I prefer a spring pole; however, both the rope and cord will work.) Of course, the amount of weight you use, as with the adjustment of pull strengths on the spring pole, needs to be appropriate for the size game you are intending to catch.

The bait pen, when used, could be made from almost anything.

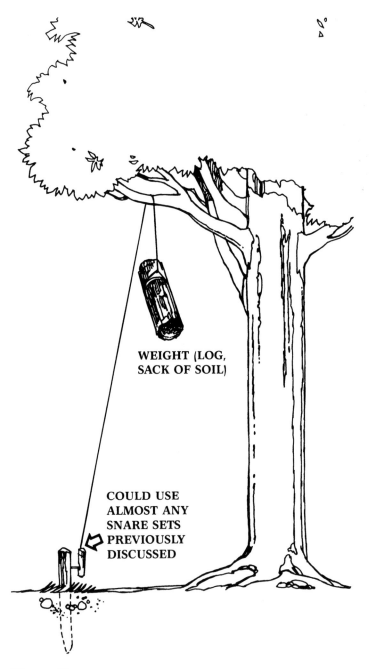

WEIGHT (LOG,
SACK OF SOIL)

COULD USE
ALMOST ANY
SNARE SETS
PREVIOUSLY
DISCUSSED

Figure 17.

The only thing I do not recommend varying is the wire lasso itself. Do not try to use rope or cord or anything that is not wire on these small snares. You can vary the thickness of the wire for different size game, but *use wire*.

There are several reasons for doing so. On small snares like these, the wire will almost hold itself up and in the correct position after you have shaped the lasso. It is also less likely to be chewed in two by a captive animal. It is strong, yet pliable. And last, but not least, the cutting nature of the copper wire tends to keep it snubbed tight around the animal with very little pull from the spring pole.

Later, in this book, cable will be used for large game like deer, but again, any size rope or cord for the lasso itself usually does not work well.

Also, do not expect to have good results if you fail to use a spring pole or weight. The anchor-to-snare system, with no jerking motion, just does not work as well as some authors and snare makers would have you believe. You may have some success with it, but you will have more success with a spring pole or weight release.

Do study the drawings shown. Endless variation is possible. Learn the details and techniques by doing! Adapt to the necessary conditions. Use whatever is available. Be creative!

Chapter 2

Large Animal Snares

Of the very few people in this country that make use of the following snare, most would call it a "deer snare." I hesitate to do so, because it is good for a wide variety of large animals. The general principle of the design will work well on deer, elk, moose, and other game of such size.

Chiefly, the motivation for setting a snare like the large animal snare is to put a large amount of meat in the freezer in one catch. The larger snares are not used as much for fur-taking.

The type of game and the motivation for snaring it call for a slightly different type of snare than we have discussed in the pest snare. The philosophy of the large animal snare is different.

Consider the wire lasso itself. Logic will tell you that on a large animal like a deer or elk, a few strands of copper wire are not going to hold him. Also, no spring pole is going to jerk such a large animal off its feet and up into the air, as this would be counterproductive even if it were possible.

What you desire in a large animal snare is one that will hold the animal or at least drastically slow down its movement from the snare site. Also, you want the

27

snare to be made so that it will not loosen and allow the animal to get its head out, but neither do you wish it to tighten to the point that it strangles the animal. Meat spoils quickly outdoors. You want the animal to be alive and healthy when you get to it. This point is important to remember because this type of snare almost always catches the animal around the neck, whereas the smaller snares rarely do.

Thus, for large animals, although the techniques are much the same, you will need a slightly different type of snare.

In northeast Texas, where all of my tinkering with snares of this type has been done, there are no elk or moose, only white-tailed deer. So, the snare set which follows will be tailored for white-tailed deer. With minor changes for different game and different game habits, you can adjust the snare for the game in your particular locality.

The first thing you must do on a whitetail snare is decide on a location. Normally, a whitetail snare is not a baited trap; extremely unusual conditions might allow you to draw deer into a snare. An example of such a situation might be a home garden with a fence around it tall enough that the deer could not jump it. If the crop in the garden was something the deer craved, such as peas, one might be able to set a snare at the gate into the garden with some success. Even more unusual conditions might allow you to draw deer to a feeder of sorts, but whitetail snares are normally set on heavily used deer trails.

You'll need to know a lot about deer trails in your neck of the woods, and you'll need a sizable population of deer in the area.

Note: Do not set a whitetail snare in an area where you see deer only once in a great while. The snare needs to be in an area where there are enough deer to be hunted fairly heavily during hunting season. The reason for this is that you need to check this snare at least every day. In an area where there are few deer, you will run yourself to death checking it every day, unless it is close to your home, and it might be quite a while before you finally catch anything.

Also, if an area is fairly well populated with deer, the trails they use are more apparent, and the chances of setting the snare in the right spot are greater.

The choice of a site is very important. If you are a hunter, watch the deer from your stand. Scout around when not in your stand for the paths you see the deer using most often. A deer trail is easy to spot once you start to really look for it. Find a spot on the trail where there is some light brush or tall weeds on each side of a well-defined trail. These weeds or brush will be used to hold the snare up from the ground and in the desired shape and position. You want your snare to be *directly on* a well-traveled white-tailed deer route, and at some point on the trail where there is some light brush or even tall weeds on each side of the trail to attach the snare to for support.

Now, with the location of your snare decided upon, you can proceed to make your snare. You will need the following items:

1   piece of cable approximately 15 to 20 feet long
3   cable clamps (2 will do in a pinch)
1   flat piece of metal with two holes
1   one-foot (or shorter) piece of string— temporary line
1   piece of spring-pole cord of appropriate length
1   log or some such drag weight

Before I get into a detailed explanation, please study Figures 18 and 19. The drawings will help clarify the word descriptions.

Armed with your general knowledge of snaring from the pest snare and after studying Figures 18 and 19, at least the general scope of the whitetail snare should be readily apparent. Looking at Figure 18, we will go over this snare piece by piece.

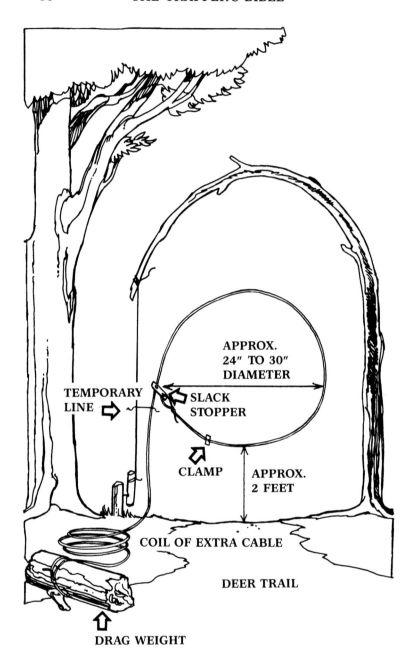

APPROX.
24" TO 30"
DIAMETER

TEMPORARY
LINE

SLACK
STOPPER

CLAMP

APPROX.
2 FEET

COIL OF EXTRA CABLE

DEER TRAIL

DRAG WEIGHT

Figure 18.

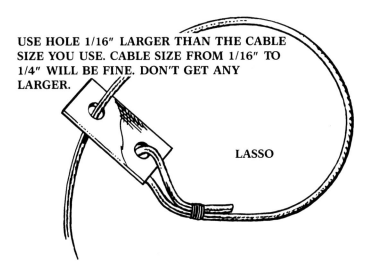

USE HOLE 1/16″ LARGER THAN THE CABLE
SIZE YOU USE. CABLE SIZE FROM 1/16″ TO
1/4″ WILL BE FINE. DON'T GET ANY
LARGER.

LASSO

Figure 19. **The principle of this whitetail snare is that once tightened, the metal slack stopper will not loosen as a simple loop would do. The slack stopper (shown above) can be made from almost any flat piece of strong metal.**

The spring pole is triggered in exactly the same way as in the pest snare. The same type of whittled peg trigger is fine. The purpose of the spring pole itself is slightly different. On a whitetail snare, the spring pole's purpose is to merely snub the snare up tight around the neck when the deer walks through the snare, bumping off the trigger. The spring pole, of course, is not supposed to jerk the deer up in the air, as in a rabbit snare, nor even to hold the deer at the snare site.

The snare itself is made from cable rather than copper wire, for obvious reasons. The diameter of the cable is not terribly important. You can use anywhere from 1/16-inch to 1/4-inch cable, but no smaller or larger than that. You will need a piece 15 to 20 feet long in order to make the lasso and have enough line left for the slack coil and to attach to the drag weight.

The purpose of the short piece of temporary line is for it to break *after* the spring pole has been triggered and the lasso has been snubbed up on the deer's neck. It should not break instantly, but should be string of such strength that when the deer begins to pull against it, it will eventually break. Kite string is about right. This will leave the deer attached to the drag weight via the cable lasso around its neck.

Note: You may have to use black electrical tape to firmly attach this temporary line to the cable just below the slack stopper.

The purpose of the slack stopper is just as the name implies. Once the snare is snubbed tight around the animal's neck, this device will prevent the cable from backing out as it would if it were merely passing through a loop in the cable. This slack stopper can be made from almost any type of metal. Scrounge around for this, as you may have to buy the cable and clamps.

The cable clamp on the line just down from the slack stopper is to keep the lasso from tightening below about six or eight inches in diameter. This will keep the deer from strangling itself as it pulls along the drag weight. Put this clamp about 12 to 14 inches down the line from the slack stopper. (*Note:* The three cable clamps are used at the slack stopper, at the point 12 to 14 inches below the slack stopper, and to attach the drag weight. Depending on what you use for a drag weight and how you attach it, you might get by without this third clamp.)

The drag weight is used for two reasons. A large animal like a white-tailed deer will fare better, and hence your meat for the freezer will be better, if it is not held fast in one spot once snared. The weight gives the deer a little freedom and it does not seem to get as upset as when held fast. I recommend about a 30-pound weight. Even less weight can be used if the weight is difficult to drag by means of its shape.

Secondly, the weight helps you to find the animal by leaving a trail behind it as it drags the weight along. The animal usually won't get far. A small log, as in Figure 18, will leave a trail easily followed.

You will also need, as stated earlier, some small brush

or weeds on each side of the trail to hold the lasso loop open and at the desired height. This brush or weed support is not shown in Figure 18.

This large animal snare is easily made and is inexpensive, even if you have to buy all of the components. It can be made with very small cable for smaller game such as foxes and coyotes. On the smaller snares, it will not always be necessary to use a drag weight. Foxes, coyotes, and the like can be held at the snare site by attaching the cable directly to the spring pole.

This snare, as with most of the traps in this book, has many possible variations for different game in different parts of the country. As with the pest snare, be creative! Good luck!

Chapter 3

Transplant Traps

Transplant traps are just what they say they are: a means of capturing an animal unharmed in order to remove it from your territory without having to destroy it.

Such traps are especially handy in neighborhood situations where you are trying to get rid of a particular pest, but would not be particularly fond of trying to explain to your neighbor how his prize poodle ended up hanging in a tree in your yard with a snare wire around its throat. A transplant trap will allow you to release any animal unharmed when necessary, while allowing you to get rid of the ones you wish.

The first transplant trap we shall look at is the net capture. You have seen it in the movies a thousand times. What they do not show you in the movies is exactly how it works. It is really very simple.

What it amounts to is a simple snare just like we have already rigged, except that instead of the snare wire going to a snare loop from the spring-pole cord, there are four cords going to the four corners of a net. See Figures 20 and 21.

The net capture is one of the few snare-like devices in which using a falling weight to jerk the net upwards

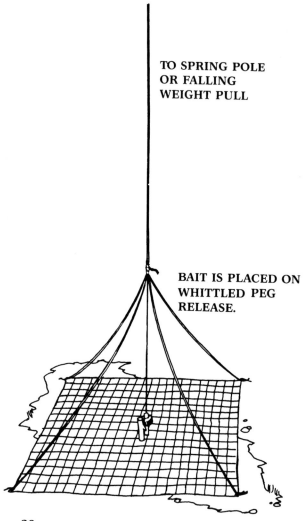

TO SPRING POLE
OR FALLING
WEIGHT PULL

BAIT IS PLACED ON
WHITTLED PEG
RELEASE.

Figure 20.

works as well, if not better, than using a spring pole.
Either will work fine with this setup, however.

The only thing that is necessary to make this work
is to make the trigger extra long (seven or eight inches)
and the stake in the ground as short as possible. You
might have to cut out one link in the net if it is made

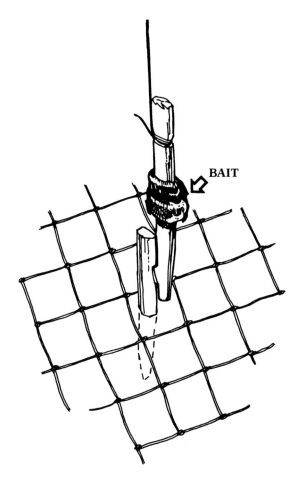

BAIT

Figure 21. **Be sure to place the net on the ground so that when it is pulled upward it will not catch on the notch of the stake in the ground. Cut one link in the net if necessary.**

of a small mesh. The slightly different trigger set (Figure 21) from our pest design, and the spacing of the net on the ground will keep the net from catching on the stake once tripped.

Obviously, the net trap is *not* like the solid box trap that we will look at next. Given time, many animals will be able to chew their way out of a net capture. Thus, such a trap needs to be checked regularly.

The next four transplant traps we will look at are all box-type capture traps. I will call them (1) armadillo, (2) pole drop, (3) pole-hinged, and (4) state of the art. They can all be homemade from a variety of materials for practically nothing dollar-wise.

ARMADILLO

The armadillo model is very common in northeast Texas. The armadillo is a scaly little critter that likes to root up your yard, dig holes, and make a general mess of your lawn. Generally speaking, it likes to do this from about ten p.m. until about three or four a.m. The armadillo trap is commonly used in Texas in an unbaited fashion to catch these destructive little devils.

First, build a box using plywood, wood planks, or some other suitable material which is about 1½ feet by 1½ feet by about 4 feet long, with each end left open. The top needs to be about one inch shorter than the sides and bottom on each end.

Using moulding of almost any kind, fashion a slideway for the doors to fall through, and make a door for each end. Build the upper support as shown in Figure 22, and string the trigger. Cut a hole in the top of the box for the trigger to rest against when set.

If you study Figure 22, the use and construction of the armadillo trap will be obvious.

Why do the armadillos go into this unbaited trap? I have no earthly idea! My only theory (and it's just a wild guess) is that due to the armadillo's very poor eyesight, it may simply bump into the trap at some time during the night. Then, in an attempt to go around the obstacle, it goes down the side and into the open end of the trap.

I do know for sure that these traps work, and work well, even though I have often been perplexed at why armadillos walk into them so willingly. It is the only box-

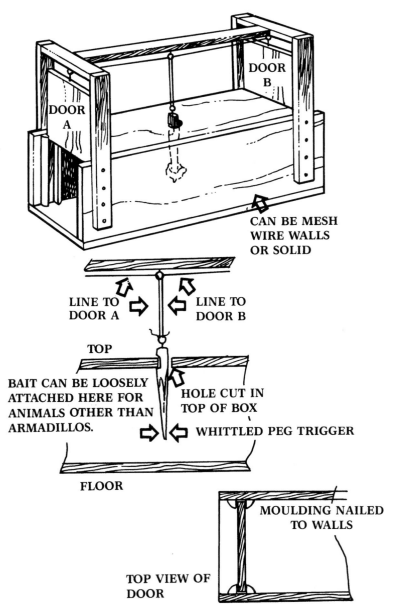

Figure 22. The principle of the armadillo trap is that the weight of the doors allows them to drop when the trigger is bumped off its catch in the hole on top of the trap.

type trap that I know of that works well unbaited, but only for armadillos. Usually, box traps are baited. This trap could be baited, and thus modified for other animals.

POLE DROP

The basic design of the pole drop is the same as the armadillo model. The difference lies in the three poles or sticks that interlock until triggered and then allow the doors to drop. It should be clear after you look at Figure 23 that when the trigger inside the box is bumped, the two top poles will be released, allowing the doors to fall. The trap is *exactly* the same as the armadillo model except for this different upper structure which is detailed in Figure 23.

POLE-HINGED

The pole-hinged model is very similar to the pole drop. The three-stick trigger assembly is identical; the box is much the same. The basic difference is that the doors do not slide down a channel; they simply slam shut somewhat like a standard doorway. They will be hinged much like a "doggy" door going into a house, except that they will work only one way, not both in and out.

Since they are hinged, the doors need a device to keep them from opening back out once the animal is inside the box; hence, the nail (see Figure 24). It is set at such an angle that the weight of the falling door will brush past the nail in closing, but will not do so when being pushed back against the nail from inside the trap. This sounds complicated, but is not.

The two sticks at the top that hold the doors up until triggered can be hooked under a small nail on the back of the doors, or any number of other ways, so that they will release when jiggled slightly, and allow the doors to fall unimpeded. Please study Figure 24.

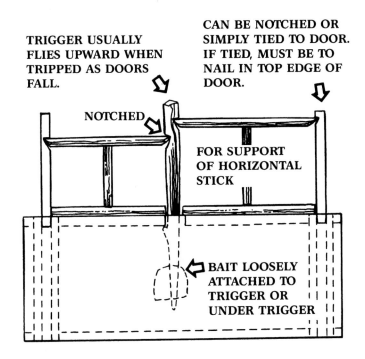

Figure 23. The upper structure is the only difference in the pole drop and the armadillo model except that the pole drop is normally baited.

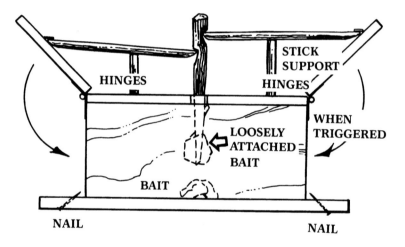

Figure 24. In the pole-hinged model, you may need to nail or otherwise attach to the back of the doors some additional weight to make the doors slam past the nails in the floor.

STATE OF THE ART

The box trap I refer to as state of the art is simplicity itself, yet it can be triggered almost by a breath of air. The bait does not even have to be tugged. The pan that holds the bait can be merely touched and the trap will spring. It can be made from almost any around-the-house-type junk, as can most of the other traps in this book.

At this point, please go back to Figure 22, our original armadillo model. The state of the art is identical except for the added bait pan and trigger inside the box. This difference makes the trap more difficult to build but also extremely sensitive to being tripped.

First, you construct a bait pan with a round wooden rod running through it. This round wooden rod is called "full round" if you have to buy it at a lumberyard. Its diameter is not very important; one inch, or less, in diameter will be about right.

The full round through the bait pan is nailed firmly in place so that when the pan is moved, the rod is twisted along with it. See Figure 25.

Next, construct the trigger assembly. It is simply a small wheel or spool around an axle of some sort, driven into the top of the full round. The example in Figure 26 shows a bent nail with some type of spool. This spool could be almost anything, as long as it will spin fairly freely on the axle you use. *Hint:* Broken appliances, especially cassette players and car stereos, have oodles of little spools inside them. Got a ruined audio cassette tape? Break it open and look inside. Even a short piece of dowel rod with a hole drilled through it lengthwise will do. See Figure 26.

Next, you make the whittled peg trigger. It needs to be a flat piece of wood (more plank than just a twig) at least twice as wide as it is thick, and long enough to extend from the trigger assembly and out the top of the box. See Figure 27.

The reason for this peg being of such dimensions is

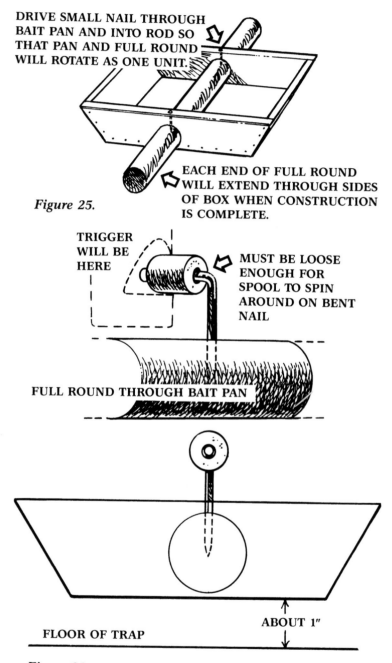

DRIVE SMALL NAIL THROUGH BAIT PAN AND INTO ROD SO THAT PAN AND FULL ROUND WILL ROTATE AS ONE UNIT.

EACH END OF FULL ROUND WILL EXTEND THROUGH SIDES OF BOX WHEN CONSTRUCTION IS COMPLETE.

Figure 25.

TRIGGER WILL BE HERE

MUST BE LOOSE ENOUGH FOR SPOOL TO SPIN AROUND ON BENT NAIL

FULL ROUND THROUGH BAIT PAN

ABOUT 1"

FLOOR OF TRAP

Figure 26.

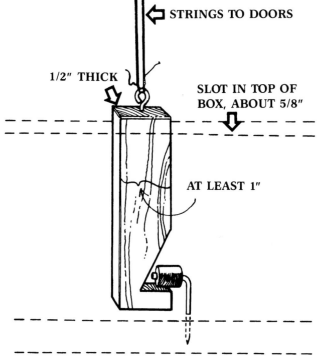

1/2" THICK

STRINGS TO DOORS

SLOT IN TOP OF
BOX, ABOUT 5/8"

AT LEAST 1"

Figure 27.

that the hole cut in the top of the trap will be cut to minimize the chances of the whittled peg catching on the top of the trap. Example: if the peg is one-half inch thick and one inch wide, make the slot in the top of the trap five-eighths inch or so. This slot can go all the way across the top. These dimensions will keep the peg from twisting and catching on the top of the box. Once tripped, the peg can do nothing but go straight up, allowing the doors to fall.

Next, the bait pan with trigger assembly connected is constructed into the box so that when the bait pan is touched, it will rotate the rod and pan one way or the other. See Figure 28.

This trap can be constructed with an extremely delicate touch. It is ideal for hard-to-catch creatures that will not spring other traps.

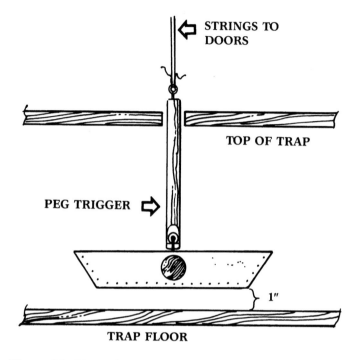

STRINGS TO
DOORS

TOP OF TRAP

PEG TRIGGER

TRAP FLOOR

1″

Figure 28. Note that any upward or downward movement of the bait pan will roll the spool off the trigger and spring the trap.

Chapter 4

Camp Alarms

At times you can feel more secure if the paths into your camp at night are set with noisemakers to let you know if someone is walking up on you.

The most handy little device I've ever run across is in the realm of fireworks. It, most simply, is a firecracker with a string coming out of each end. When either end is pulled, the firecracker explodes. You do not have to light it with a match or a lighter of any kind. These fireworks are cheap. They sell for about a dime a box, and a box contains twelve. I do not see how they are made so cheaply, much less retailed for that price. They are sold under different names, but most people call them booby traps. At Christmas and other holidays, I stock up. You can buy hundreds of them for two or three dollars.

In case the use of these booby traps is not apparent to you by now, this is how they can be used as a primitive alarm system. Run a string across any likely paths into your camp. Tie one end firmly on one side of the path to whatever solid object is available (tree, stake, limb, etc.)

On the other end, tie the string to one of the strings on the booby trap. Tie the string on the other end of the booby trap to something solid on that side of the path. Set the string across the path so that it is about one foot from the ground and fairly taut.

When someone comes down the path during the night, his foot will catch on the string, jerking it and exploding the firecracker. If one of these booby traps is not loud enough, tie six or eight together in the same fashion. The more the merrier!

These booby traps will have to be bought, as opposed to being homemade as most of the things in this book are. I suspect that they may be difficult to make yourself. But, they are so cheap, why bother? Buy some when the time is right, since they might not be readily available when you actually need them.

There is an added benefit to these alarms. In addition to letting you know of an intruder, they are great for scaring off the weak at heart. A would-be bad guy coming into your camp for no good reason would likely have second thoughts if six or eight (or a dozen) firecrackers explode three feet away in the dark when he trips the trip wire. See Figure 29.

If you wish to set a firmer lesson for your intruder, do this. Tie a wire or strong cord tightly across the path into your camp, firmly attached to objects on both sides. Then, place a log (or whatever you want your intruder to fall into) just past the trip wire.

If, during the night, an intruder doesn't see the wire and trips, he will most likely catch his teeth on the log you have set a few feet past the wire. I prefer the booby trap, myself. It just depends on the situation and how serious you feel the threat against you to be. How serious the threat is can determine what you set beyond the wire for the intruder to fall on.

The old standby is the barbed wire and tin can routine. You have seen this in a thousand war movies. To use this, you would really have to be in almost a war-type setting. It is a lot of trouble and is expensive if you do not just happen to have a lot of barbed wire around.

You can string the wire with the tin cans attached all

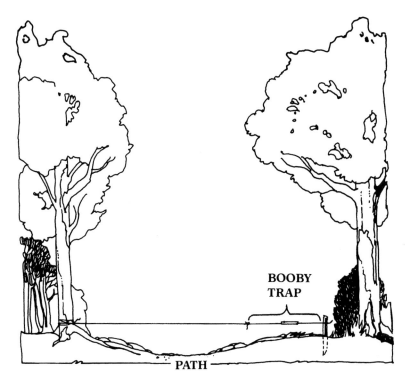

Figure 29. **For a more effective noisemaker, tie six or eight booby traps instead of just one.**

the way around the perimeter of your camp or just on the paths into your camp. The wire needs to be in tangled coils so that someone cannot just step through it like they would a barbed wire fence. Use *lots* of cans. Theoretically, when someone gets his clothes caught on the barbs trying to slip through, it will jiggle the whole mess, rattling the cans. *Note:* do not try to use this method only on the paths into your camp unless other routes into your camp are a sheer rock cliff or something on that order. Unlike the trip wire shown earlier, your intruder will usually see this barrier of barbed wire and cans as the coils need to be about three feet high to be effective. In most cases, if using this method, you will need to use it all the way around your camp. If your situation is this desperate, do a good job.

The tin can alarm I like best is the tin can snare. It is very much like our pest snare except that it jerks up (or drops) a wired-up blob of about 20 tin cans, making a heck of a racket.

Set a stake in the ground with a nail in it, and rig a whittled peg release as we did in Figure 3. Run the cord over a limb and tie it to about 20 tin cans instead of running it to a spring pole. String a trip line across it to the whittled peg. *Loosely* is the key word in the last sentence. See Figure 30.

When the trip line is tripped, the cans will fall with a loud racket. You can even have them fall on your intruder if there is a convenient limb available. For that matter, if the situation were desperate enough, you could have it drop something other than tin cans on him. That will be left to your discretion.

You can reverse the procedure if you wish. Instead of the tin cans dangling in the air as in Figure 30, put a weight in their place. Then, on the ground, tie the coil of tin cans to the whittled peg release so that when the wire is tripped, the cans go up, rattling all the way.

There are a lot of things like those mentioned here that will keep you alert to someone intruding in your area. These are all relatively harmless to your intruder— certainly not fatal, barring some accident. The barbed-wire treatment might not thrill your adversary, but odds are he would live through it.

This may not be true with the traps described in the following chapter. The chapter, simply titled, "Last Resort Traps," details dangerous pathguarders. They should be used *only* in a desperate effort to save your life. Treat this chapter with respect. If your situation gets to this point, it has long since passed the point of being a game.

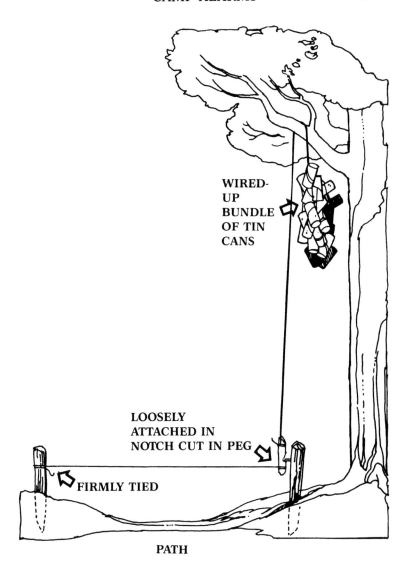

WIRED-
UP
BUNDLE
OF TIN
CANS

LOOSELY
ATTACHED IN
NOTCH CUT IN PEG

FIRMLY TIED

PATH

Figure 30.

Chapter 5

Last Resort Traps

There may come a time when snaring game for food may not be enough to enable you to stay alive. You may have to prevent armed men from entering your territory, or, at least, slow them down if they are in pursuit of you and your party. It is hoped that you or I will never have to experience this. But, you never know.

The traps shown in this chapter are dangerous. Treat them with respect. *Never set one of these traps except to save your life.* That is the *only* reason they are included in this book. There is always some idiot out there who thinks it might be really "cool" to set one of these. For that reason, I hesitated to include them in this book. Don't be an idiot!

PUNJI #1

A heavily used pathguarding trap in Vietnam was one made of punji sticks in the bottom of a shallow pit which was covered over to make it appear like solid ground. Punji sticks are simply sharpened pieces of bamboo, though any type of sharpened stick can be used. (Bamboo was convenient in Vietnam.) The sticks were placed in these foot traps with the sharp end pointing up and the other end driven into the ground. They were dipped in human excrement so that the wound caused would become infected. See Figure 31.

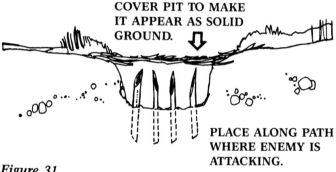

COVER PIT TO MAKE
IT APPEAR AS SOLID
GROUND.

PLACE ALONG PATH
WHERE ENEMY IS
ATTACKING.

Figure 31.

PUNJI #2

After "Charlie" learned that the Vietnam-style boots American GIs wore were at least halfway puncture-resistant and had high tops, they started setting the punji traps to work above the top of the boots.

Figure 32 shows the basic trap except that the punji sticks face downward at an angle. When you step into the hole, your foot goes down in all the way. The normal reaction will be to jerk your leg back up. This will cause the sharpened spears to puncture the leg, *above* the boot top.

PIT COVERED TO APPEAR SOLID

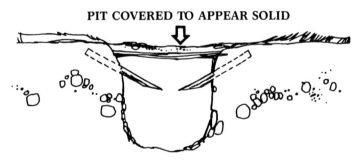

Figure 32.

PUNJI #3

Figure 33 shows the same basic trap, except that it uses two wood blocks with nails to clamp onto the leg above the boot top as the foot pushes down past the first level of the trap.

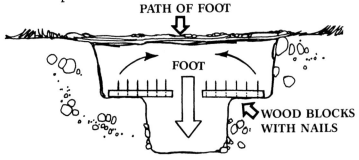

Figure 33.

THE BOW AND ARROW PATHGUARDER

It has been mentioned, pertaining to several traps in this book, that you have seen them in a thousand movies. If that is true of the other traps, then this one has been in a million movies and TV shows. The ultimate fear inducer—the bow and arrow pathguarder.

The bow and arrow pathguarder takes a little longer to set than a snare, but the simplicity of the trap is amazing. In actuality, it is somewhat like a snare; it just throws an arrow instead of jerking a snare wire. It does not even matter which direction the victim is walking on the path. It works both ways.

First, build a bow of whatever strength you feel necessary. Keep in mind, when making this bow, that the properties of springiness that we discussed earlier in relation to the spring pole are essential to this bow as well. Make some arrows out of bamboo, cane, or whatever is available.

Find a bend in the path you wish to guard and set the trap as shown in Figure 34. Examples of arrows are

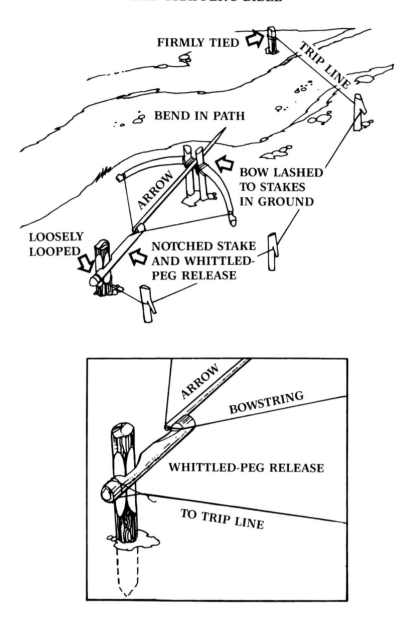

Figure 34. Note that how you set the elevation of the aim is determined by the height at which the bow is lashed to the stakes, the trigger-stake height, and the lay of the terrain.

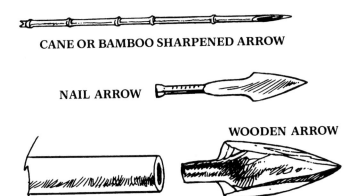

CANE OR BAMBOO SHARPENED ARROW

NAIL ARROW

WOODEN ARROW

SAME ARROW AS ABOVE EXCEPT WITH
WHITTLED-WOOD ARROWHEAD CARVED TO FIT
IN HOLLOW END OF BAMBOO OR CANE. SEAR
ARROWHEAD WITH FIRE TO HARDEN. CAN
ALSO USE HAMMER-FLATTENED NAIL FILED TO
SAME SHAPE FOR ARROWHEAD. USE MUD TO
FIRMLY DRY NAIL IN BAMBOO END.

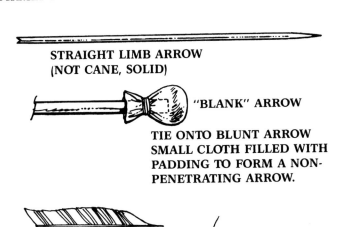

STRAIGHT LIMB ARROW
(NOT CANE, SOLID)

"BLANK" ARROW

TIE ONTO BLUNT ARROW
SMALL CLOTH FILLED WITH
PADDING TO FORM A NON-
PENETRATING ARROW.

Figure 35. Fletching (feathers) can be glued onto any
of these arrow designs, if desired and if materials are
available.

shown in Figure 35. The type of arrow you use depends on your seriousness of intent and on the materials available.

The degree of damage to the victim can be heightened or lessened to no damage at all by the following three things:

1. The strength of the bow. Generally speaking, the harder any particular arrow hits a target, the more damage it will do. As with the spring pole mentioned previously, the strength of any bow can be varied to some degree simply by how far back you pull it. However, this adjustment is not as great with a bow as it is with a spring pole.

2. The arrow you use. There may be times when you merely want to scare some trespasser off your land, and you do not wish to hurt anyone even slightly. In such an instance, use the "blank" arrow in Figure 35. Use it in conjunction with a *weak* bow. Even a blank arrow could do damage with a strong bow if it struck someone in the face. Use just enough bow strength to hurl the arrow toward the trip line—just enough to get the intruder's attention. He is sure to find the bow after the arrow whizzes by. You might even add a note next to the bow that says, "You could've been dead, boy!"

3. The height at which the arrow is aimed. Obvious reasoning.

THE STABBER

A stabber is another type of pathguarding trap that can be very deadly. Or, it can be set so that when tripped it is only a warning to a trespasser of what could have happened.

Pick a spot where two trees are growing close together near the path. Cut a springy sapling with the same features as for a spring pole. Lash the pole to the two trees so that the end of the sapling reaches to at least the center of the path at whatever height would be correct for your victim.

Next, lash a sharpened stick, sharpened bamboo, or whatever you can scrounge up for the stabbing blade, to the end of the stabber arm. Mark the spot below the stabber on the path. This is the point where the trip line will cross the path. Then, bend the pole back as far as you can. Look down and make note of how far you pulled it back. Three or four feet behind this point, you will set the trigger. Figures 36 and 37 will show you the

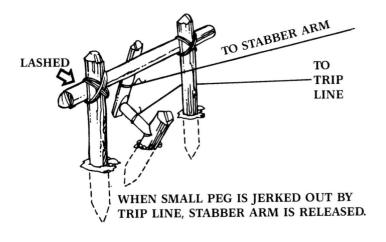

LASHED

TO STABBER ARM

TO TRIP LINE

WHEN SMALL PEG IS JERKED OUT BY TRIP LINE, STABBER ARM IS RELEASED.

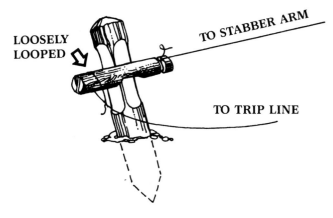

LOOSELY LOOPED

TO STABBER ARM

TO TRIP LINE

Figure 36. **This illustration depicts two different trigger sets you can use.**

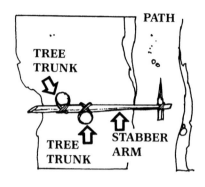

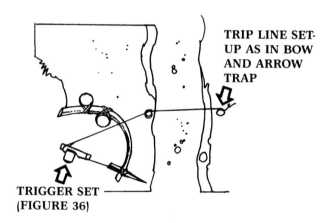

Figure 37. **The topmost illustration shows the layout of an unset stabber (a top view), while the lower illustration is the layout of a set stabber.**

trigger set and the layout of the stabber, respectively.

The damage the stabber does to the victim can be heightened or lessened by the following variables:

1. The blade. The length of the blade attached to the stabber arm can obviously make a difference. Also, the number of blades could be increased to four or five along the last two feet of the arm, and the trap wouldn't miss.

Also, on the stabber arm, it is not imperative to have an actual blade. If you have a pesky trespasser that you want to catch in the act, a healthy swat from the stabber arm about knee level can do wonders even without the sharp blade. Therefore, the blade variable can make all the difference in the world, even if the other variables remain constant.

2. The pull strength of the stabber arm. This can make a difference in the amount of damage done by whatever you are using on the end of the arm. Even if you use no blade whatever, the arm could be made so strong that it would break a leg, or so weak that it would merely swat your victim.

3. The height of the arm. Where the arm strikes the victim will make a difference one way or the other, depending on whether you have set it at a height to catch the vitals or the ankles.

Afterword

Please learn the secrets of snaring. It is a cheap and useful technique for obtaining food when your equipment is limited and the chips are down. This book has been compiled from practical experience and years of learning. Most bookstores do not have books on this subject. I hope you enjoy this one.

To obtain information on more modern methods of trapping, survival, and the deterrence of enemies, I recommend two sources.

The first is magazines such as *Outdoor Life* and *Field and Stream*. This type of magazine usually advertises modern traps as well as books on trapping. Magazines such as *Soldier of Fortune* will have ads on trapping, plus many other survival-related subjects.

The second source is Paladin Press in Boulder, Colorado. It publishes books on almost any subject that has to do with staying alive in this old world. Its ads can be found in magazines like *Soldier of Fortune,* and many other places.